STAGE 3

BOOK 3

BIRTHDAY GIRL

John Townsend

RISING ★ STARS

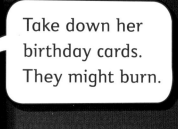

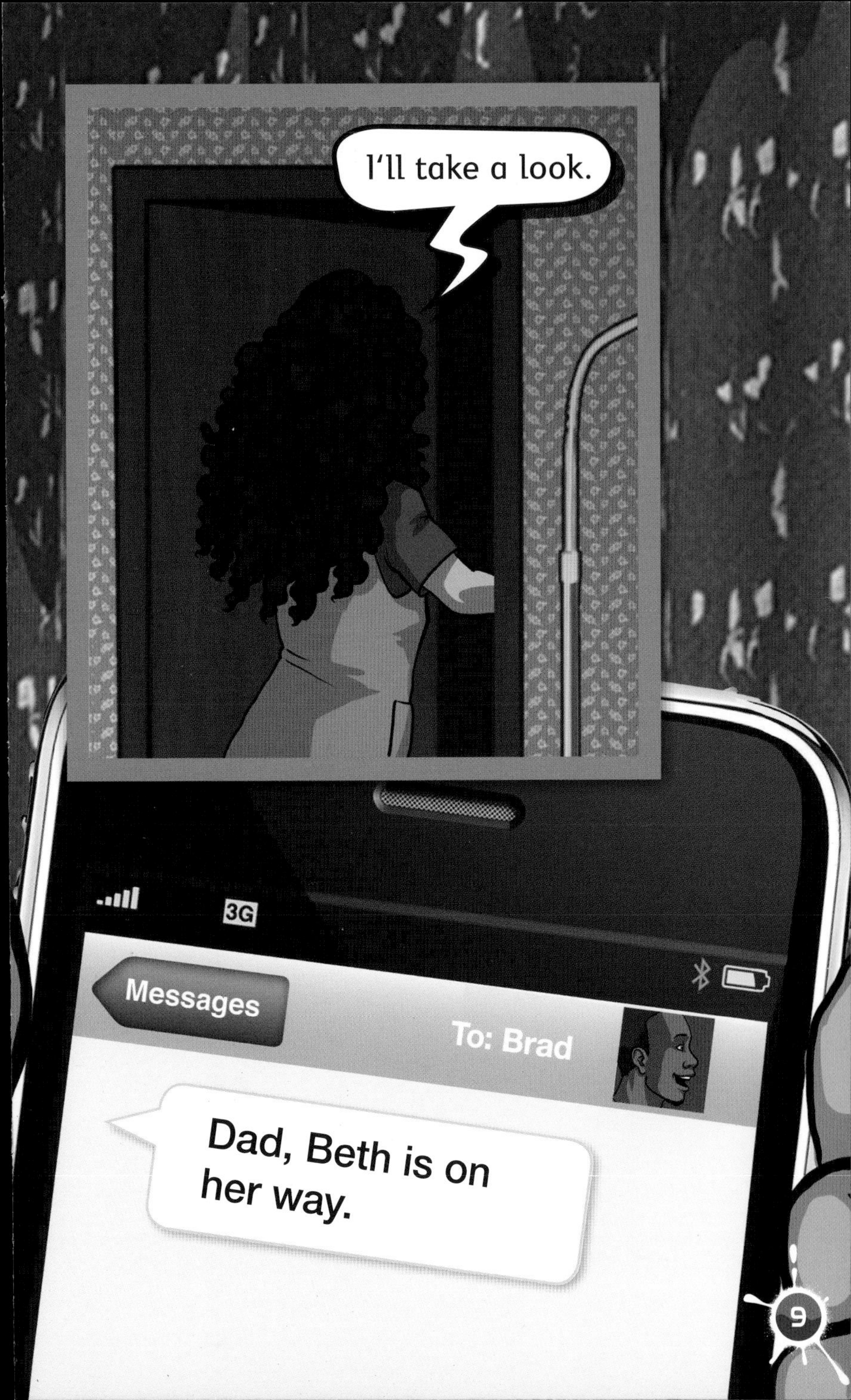
I'll take a look.
Messages
3G
To: Brad
Dad, Beth is on her way.

CHECK

1. Why was Beth unhappy on her birthday?

2. What did Taz say to make her feel better?

3. How did Mum try to make her feel better?

4. What did Taz say was making the sound?

5. What was the secret that made Beth feel better?

FIND

Find the words to fill the gaps.

1. It was a _____ winter's night.   (page 2)

2. He's made Beth's room look so _____ .
(page 11)

3. _____ birthday!   (page 11)

What's missing?

1. turn up the heater taz   (page 2)

2. dad didnt send her a card or even a text   (page 4)

3. ssh … whats that sound   (page 6)

Put the **verbs** *(burn, curl, turn) in the right gaps.*

1. _____ up the heater, Taz.   (page 2)

2. They might _____ .   (page 3)

3. Just let me _____ up by the heater.   (page 6)

Which word in the story means

1. pull a face or scowl?   (page 3)

2. upset?   (page 5)

3. noise?   (page 6)

4. in need of a drink?   (page 12)

*Swap the word in **bold** for a new word that means the opposite.*

5. It was **loud**.

6. Do you feel **more** like a birthday girl now?